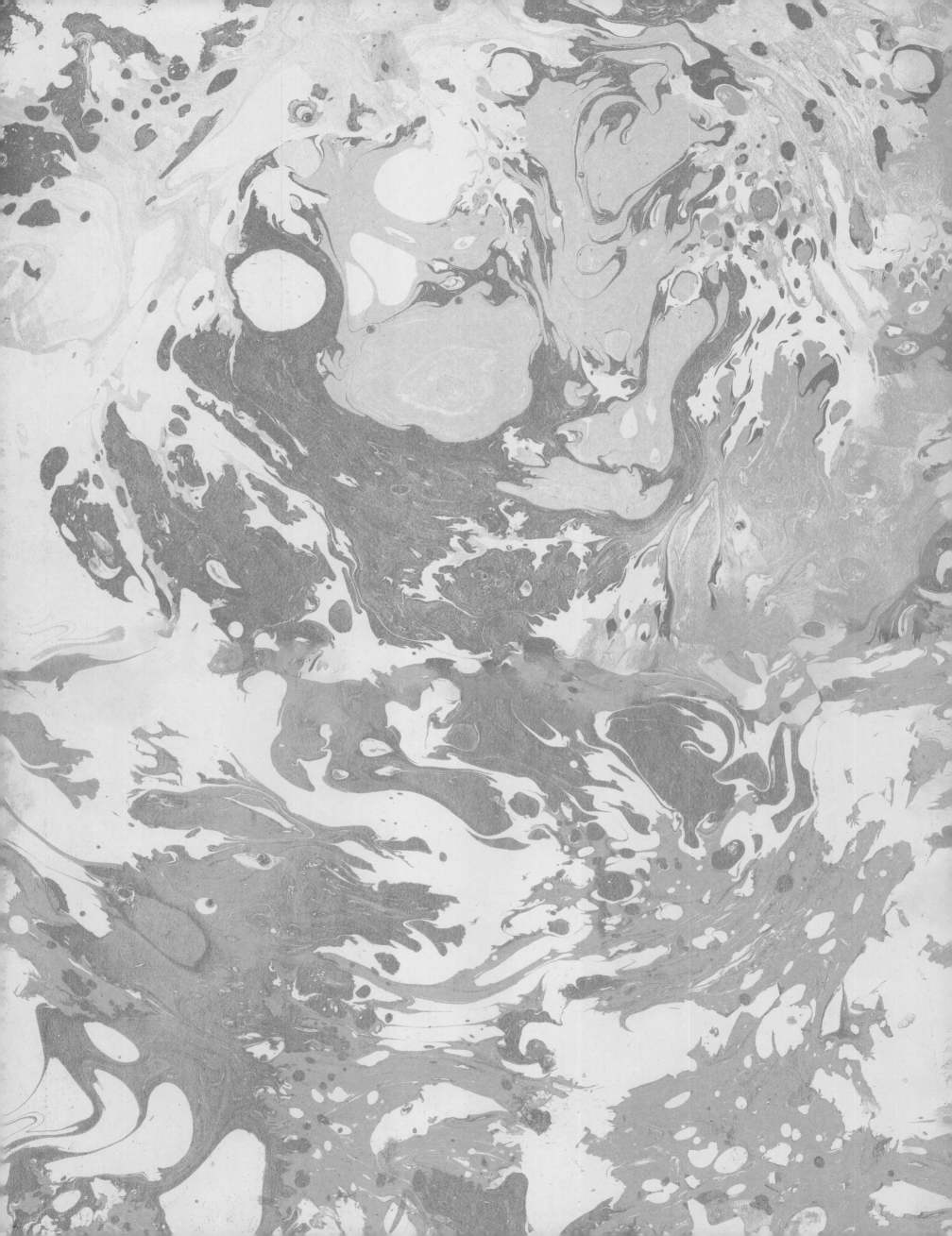

GLOW

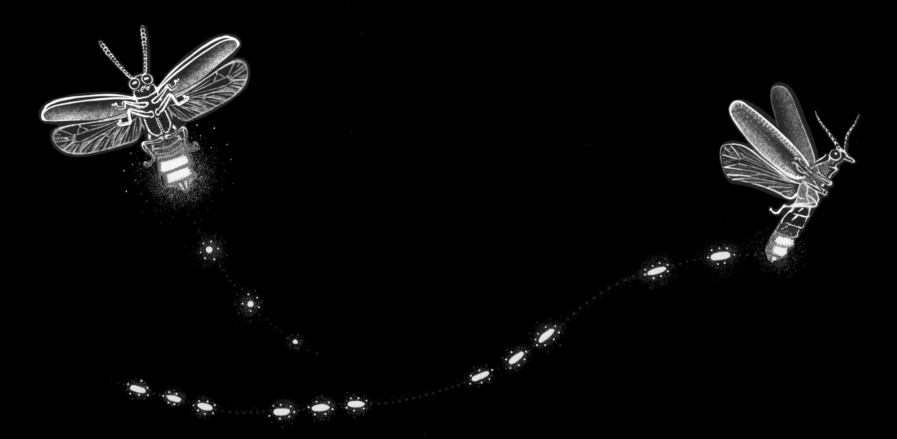

To Rosemary in the early 1970s, pretending to scuba dive in her garden.
To Beatrice in the early 1940s, cycling home with her path lit by glowworms.
To my mother and grandmother, and all children who are like them.—J.S.

Glow © 2023 Thames & Hudson Ltd, London
Text and illustrations © 2023 Jennifer N. R. Smith

Consultancy by Dr. Edith Widder

First published in the United States of America in 2023
by Thames & Hudson Inc., 500 Fifth Avenue, New York,
New York 10110

Library of Congress Control Number 2022945838

ISBN 978-0-500-65320-3

Printed in China by Artron Art (Group) Co., Ltd.

Be the first to know about our new releases,
exclusive content and author events by visiting
thamesandhudson.com
thamesandhudsonusa.com
thamesandhudson.com.au

JENNIFER N. R. SMITH

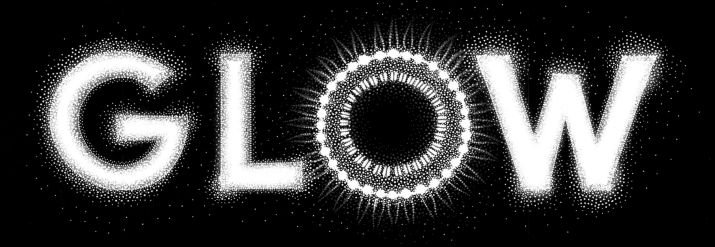

GLOW

the WILD WONDERS *of* BIOLUMINESCENCE

CONTENTS

WILDLIFE

SPARKLES AND GLOWS

IT'S A WARM SUMMER EVENING AT THE BEACH AND THE SUN HAS JUST GONE DOWN.
Out of the corner of your eye, you notice the waves flashing strangely in the twilight. You
realize it's not just your imagination. You walk closer to the sea and crouch down, drawing your
hand through the water. As you disturb it, a curious blue light follows. You raise your hand
from under the surface, and tiny stars sparkle and then fade across your skin.

As the night draws in, your surroundings darken—but the water becomes even more vibrant.
A magical blue light glows and fades with the cresting and breaking of the waves. As you walk
away from the water's edge, your footsteps on the wet sand light up beneath you. This phenomenon
is known as "sea sparkle," and is an example of . . .

BIOLUMINESCENCE

"Bio" means living. "Luminescence" is a type of light.
So bioluminescence means living light.

Bioluminescence is the emission of light caused by chemical reactions inside certain animals,
fungi, and bacteria. It makes these creatures glow. From fireflies to jellyfish, bioluminescence
comes in different forms and has many functions in the natural world.

Creatures are rarely bioluminescent for just one reason and they often use their ability in
a variety of ways. These include defense, luring **prey**, communicating, attracting a **mate**, and
camouflage. "Sea sparkle" is caused by tiny **microorganisms** called **dinoflagellates**, which light
up when they are disturbed. Many kinds of dinoflagellate can create this magical effect,
including one called *Noctiluca scintillans,* which is illustrated on the opposite page.

PLATE KEY

1. DOLPHINS swimming in the sea sparkle, leaving trails of light
2. MAUVE STINGER JELLYFISH
3. SEA SPARKLE under the microscope—*Noctiluca scintillans*
4. MAUVE STINGER JELLYFISH viewed from above

1.

2.

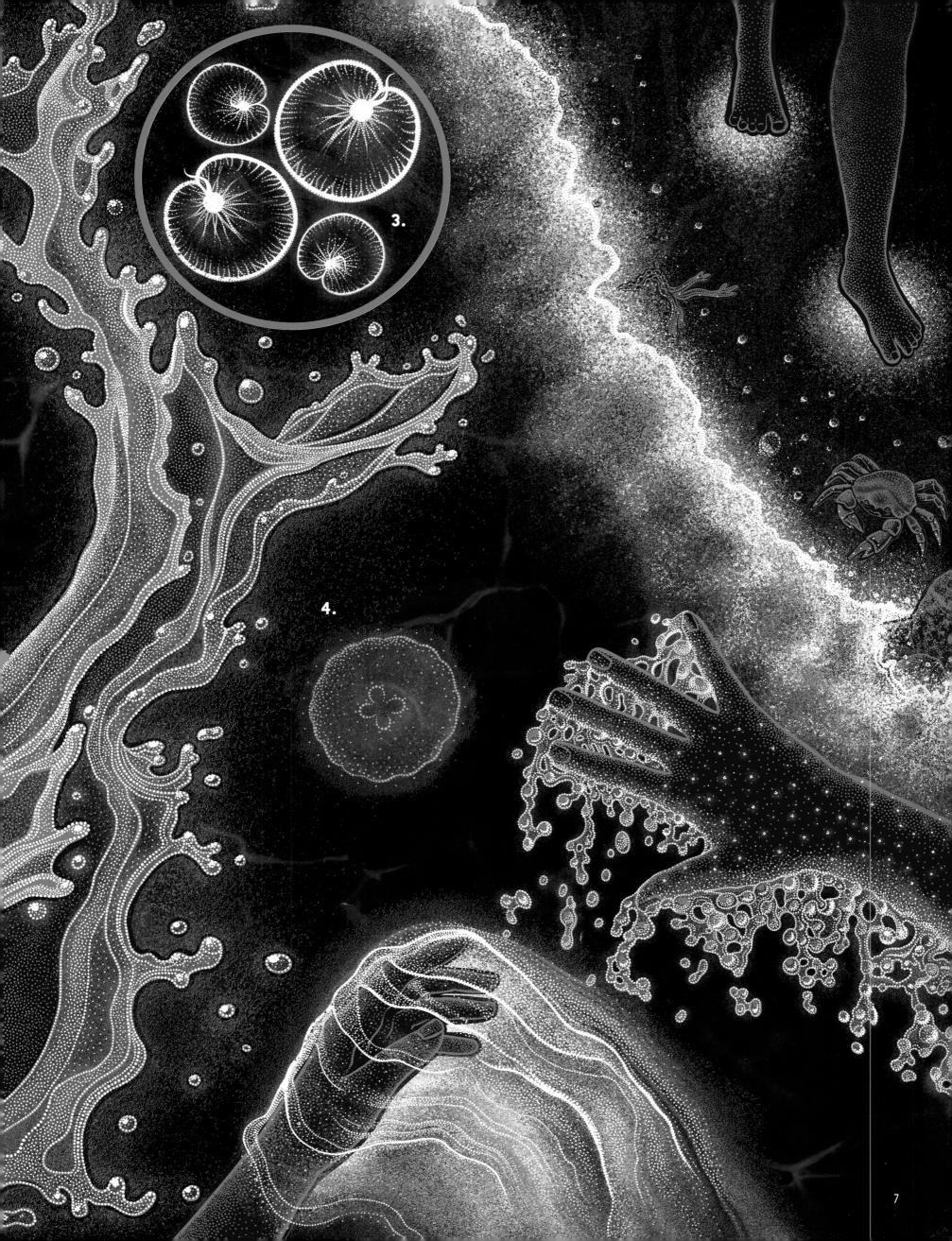

A LANGUAGE OF LIGHT

BIOLUMINESCENCE CAN BE A WAY FOR CREATURES TO COMMUNICATE.

Have you ever spotted tiny lights in the bushes, or floating in the night sky?
If so, you might have witnessed glowworms or fireflies sending each other messages.

WHAT'S IN A NAME?

Fireflies are not actually flies and glowworms are not actually worms! Almost all of them are beetles. Glowworm is the name given to some types of wingless female fireflies and young **larvae**. The larval stage is a stage of growth that many insects go through between hatching from an egg and becoming an adult. These beetle larvae look kind of like worms with glowing butts.

EUROPEAN GLOWWORM *Lampyris noctiluca*

LANTERN

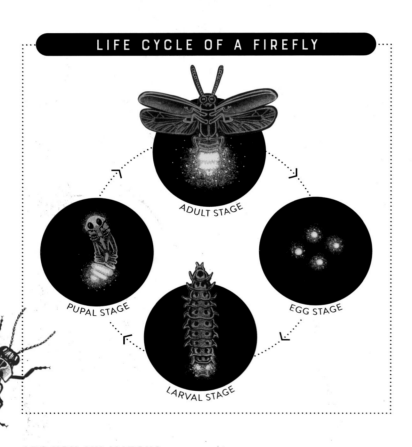

LIFE CYCLE OF A FIREFLY

ADULT STAGE

PUPAL STAGE

EGG STAGE

LARVAL STAGE

I'M OVER HERE!

Many fireflies and glowworms glow to attract a **mate**. Some flash and others glow continuously, such as the European glowworm, *Lampyris noctiluca*. The female European glowworm is wingless and glows. The male has wings but doesn't glow. The female twists her glowing body or "**lantern**" up toward the sky. The male sees the female's light and flies toward her.

ARE YOU MY MATCH?

Some fireflies flash in patterns that are specific to their species—this helps them find one another. They are nicknamed "lightning bugs." Other fireflies, such as *Photinus carolinus*, synchronize their flashing when they all get together in a **swarm**—like a bioluminescent flash mob!

PLEASED TO EAT YOU

The "femme fatale" firefly, *Photuris pensylvanica*, uses its glow to deceive other species. It copies the flashing patterns that *Photinus* fireflies use to attract a male. The male is tricked into thinking it has found a mate from its own species but instead the female "femme fatale" firefly eats it as **prey**!

"FEMME FATALE" FIREFLY *Photuris pensylvanica*

PLATE KEY

FLASH PATTERNS OF LIGHTNING BUGS IN NORTH AMERICA
1. *PHOTINUS CONSIMILIS* **2.** *PHOTINUS PYRALIS*
3. *PHOTINUS IGNITUS* **4.** *PHOTINUS GRANULATUS* **5.** *PHOTINUS MARGINELLUS*

DINNER IN THE DEEP

OUR OCEANS ARE BRIMMING WITH GLOWING LIFE.
An incredible 76% of marine creatures are bioluminescent.

The ocean can be divided into three environmental zones, each with a different level of light. The **sunlight zone** is the brightest—from the water's surface down to 650 feet deep. Between 650 and 3,300 feet deep is the darker **twilight zone**. Beyond 3,300 feet is the **midnight zone**, which is so deep that no light reaches it from the surface. Most bioluminescent creatures live in the twilight and midnight zones. Some move between the three, depending on the time of day. As you can imagine, living in the dark can make it tricky to spot your next meal.

CAUGHT IN THE HEADLIGHTS
The splitfin flashlight fish has patches under its eyes that light up like headlights. They are **nocturnal** and make a daily **migration** from the twilight zone where they live during the day, to the sunlight zone where they hunt at night. Scientists think they flash their patches to communicate with each other and to search for prey.

SPLITFIN FLASHLIGHT FISH *Anomalops katoptron*

GLOWING SUCKER OCTOPUS *Stauroteuthis syrtensis*

LURING WITH LIGHT
Some creatures use bioluminescence to lure their prey toward them—and to guide dinner into their mouths! The glowing sucker octopus flashes its glowing suckers to attract copepods—tiny crustaceans—toward its beak.

ESCA

ILLICIUM

DEEP-SEA ANGLERFISH *Melanocetus johnsonii*

GLOWING FISHING ROD
The deep-sea anglerfish has a long, thin stalk on the top of its head—like a fishing rod with a light on the tip. The rod is called the **illicium** and the light, or lure, is called the **esca**. The anglerfish can move it in any direction, and can wiggle it around to act as bait to the anglerfish's prey.

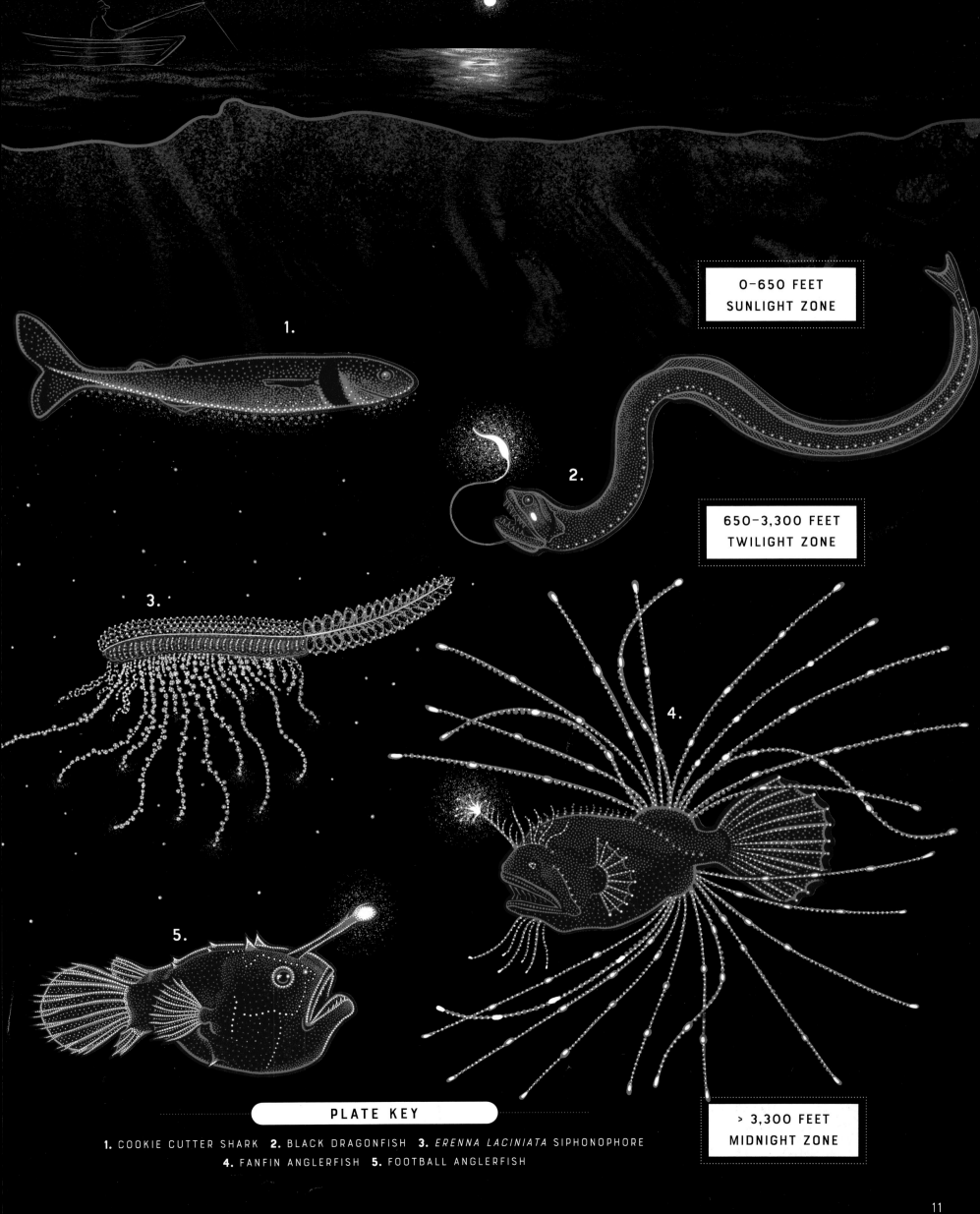

0-650 FEET
SUNLIGHT ZONE

650-3,300 FEET
TWILIGHT ZONE

> 3,300 FEET
MIDNIGHT ZONE

PLATE KEY

1. COOKIE CUTTER SHARK **2.** BLACK DRAGONFISH **3.** *ERENNA LACINIATA* SIPHONOPHORE
4. FANFIN ANGLERFISH **5.** FOOTBALL ANGLERFISH

A STRATEGY OF DEFENSE

BEING A DEEP-SEA CREATURE IS DANGEROUS.

If you don't have a smart defensive strategy like bioluminescence,
you could easily become another creature's dinner.

....

BAMBOO CORAL *Keratoisis flexibilis*

INTRUDER ALERT!

Some creatures give off light when they are threatened, like
a burglar alarm. Bamboo coral such as *Keratoisis flexibilis* does
exactly this—it wards off its enemies by producing brilliant
neon-blue flashes when it is disturbed. The *Atolla* jellyfish sets
off a spectacular pinwheel of light when it is under attack. The
light draws the attention of even bigger predators, which hunt
the creatures that are hunting the *Atolla* jellyfish!

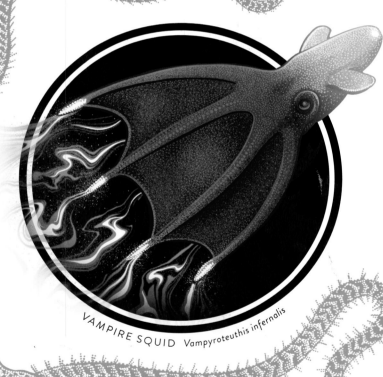

VAMPIRE SQUID *Vampyroteuthis infernalis*

NOW YOU SEE ME . . .

Now you don't! Many species use bioluminescence to dazzle and
confuse their predators. One example is the deep-sea-dwelling
vampire squid. You probably know some species of squid spray
ink at their attackers to blind them temporarily. The defensive
strategy of the vampire squid is similar but instead of ink, it has
adapted to squirt a glowing mucus. This distracts the attacker while
the squid makes a quick getaway. But it gets worse—the mucus
sticks to the attacker and attracts larger predators to the scene!

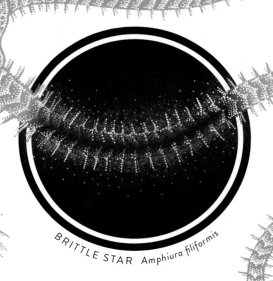

BRITTLE STAR *Amphiura filiformis*

A DEVIOUS DECOY

The brittle star is a close relative of starfish and has five long,
flexible limbs. When it comes under attack, the brittle star can
escape by sacrificing a limb. It voluntarily detaches it and the
predator is tricked into following the limb, which continues to flash
on its own while the brittle star escapes. Some deep-sea creatures
are transparent, so if a see-through predator eats a flashing limb,
it will itself become a glowing target for other predators. Even
better, the brittle star is able to grow back any missing limbs!

PLATE KEY

1. *ATOLLA* JELLYFISH **2.** HELMET JELLYFISH **3.** FIRE-BREATHING SHRIMP **4.** SEA FIREFLY
5. BUBBLEGUM CORAL **6.** VENUS FLYTRAP ANEMONE **7.** BRITTLE STAR **8.** BAMBOO CORAL

THE **BRIGHTEST**
CAMOUFLAGE

IMAGINE YOU'RE A HUNGRY DEEP-SEA PREDATOR LOOKING FOR YOUR DINNER.
The sun is streaming down through the water above you. Below you, the ocean looks dark and murky.
You're more likely to find a tasty fish by looking up toward the surface at fish whose shadows
are clearly outlined than by looking down into the darkness below.

Now imagine you are a fish trying to avoid being that predator's next meal.
How do you avoid making your shadow visible? Shine a bright light from your belly!
Your belly light will blend in with the strong light coming from the water's surface.

This brilliant technique is called **COUNTER-ILLUMINATION**. It's a
favorite of bioluminescent fish, squid, and shrimp that live in the upper ocean.

HAWAIIAN BOBTAIL SQUID Euprymna scolopes

ALWAYS WATCHING
The spooky-looking barrel eye fish has a
transparent forehead and highly sensitive
eyes that filter green light. This may allow
it to tell the difference between sunlight
and bioluminescence, and to catch
creatures using counter-illumination.

PLAINFIN MIDSHIPMAN Porichthys notatus

HIDING IN PLAIN SIGHT
Some predators use counter-
illumination to sneak up on prey.
The bobtail squid uses bioluminescent
bacteria to light up its belly. This
camouflages the squid as it descends
toward delicious shrimp living down
below, on the sea bed.

BARREL EYE FISH Macropinna microstoma

A LIVING DIMMER SWITCH
The organs that produce the light
for counter-illumination are called
photophores. They can be switched
on and off, or even dimmed or
brightened! This allows a creature
to match the light from above more
closely and improve its camouflage.

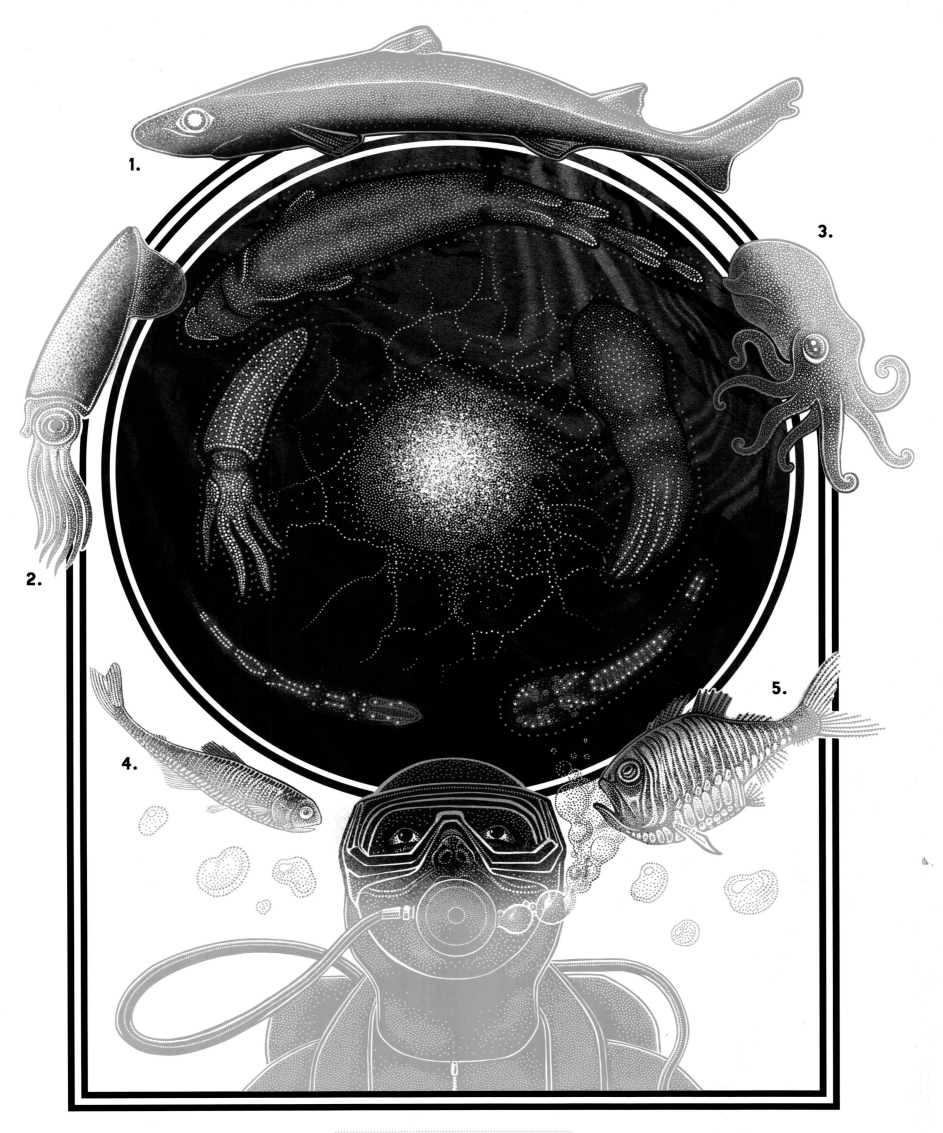

PLATE KEY

1. VELVET BELLY LANTERNSHARK **2.** FIREFLY SQUID **3.** HAWAIIAN BOBTAIL SQUID
4. LANTERNFISH **5.** HATCHET FISH

FUNGAL FAIRY LIGHTS

GLOWING MUSHROOMS SEEM LIKE THEY SHOULD ONLY BELONG IN FAIRY TALES.

Yet they are real and can be found around the world. So far, we know of about 100 species
of fungi that give off their own light—and new species are still being discovered.

WHY DO SOME FUNGI GLOW?

Have you noticed how some insects can't help but buzz toward a
source of light? Scientists think that bioluminescent fungi glow
precisely for this reason—to attract insects. When an insect
crawls over the fungi, it becomes covered in fungal **spores**, which
are the particles that fungi use to reproduce. The insect spreads
the spores wherever it travels next, planting new fungi as it goes.

FLOR DE COCO *Neonothopanus gardneri*

KEEPING AN EYE ON THE TIME

Many species of fungi give off a continuous glow, day and
night. But some species, such as *Neonothopanus gardneri* or
the Flor de Coco fungus, stop glowing during the day when
bioluminescence is no longer visible.

COME DINE WITH ME?

Just because a mushroom is bioluminescent, that doesn't mean it
is **toxic** (although you should never eat any mushrooms you find,
unless you are a trained forager). However, some scientists think that
mushrooms glow to discourage would-be diners. This is because the
glow would draw attention to the scene and attract bigger predators—
and the bigger predators might then eat the mushroom-eater!

THE STRUCTURE OF A MUSHROOM

FRUITING
BODY

HYPHAE

THALLUS

MYCELIUM

The round top of a mushroom is called the **fruiting body**—
this is where spores are produced. The stalk is called the
thallus. The inside of a mushroom is made up of stringy
fibers called **hyphae**. The hyphae are tangled together in a
complex network called the **mycelium**, which extends from
the inside of a mushroom to the underground, like roots.

In some species of fungi, such as *Armillaria mellea* or
honey fungus, only the mycelium glows. The mycelium
is not usually visible so we are not sure why it glows—this
puzzle remains unsolved.

HONEY FUNGUS *Armillaria mellea*

PLATE KEY

1. BLEEDING FAIRY HELMET **2.** *FILOBOLETUS MANIPULARIS* **3.** ETERNAL LIGHT MUSHROOM **4.** LITTLE PING-PONG BATS
5. BITTER OYSTER **6.** GREEN PEPE **7.** JACK-O'-LANTERN **8.** GHOST MUSHROOM

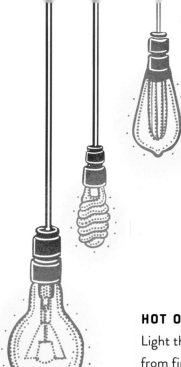

TYPES OF LIGHT

BIOLUMINESCENCE IS OFTEN MISTAKENLY CALLED PHOSPHORESCENCE.

If that's not confusing enough, there's also biofluorescence.

So which one is which and what are the differences?

....

HOT OR COLD?

Light that comes from heat is called **incandescence**. Light from fire, the sun, and most light bulbs is incandescent light.

Light that is made without heat is called **luminescence**. It is also known as "cold light." **Bioluminescence**, **biofluorescence**, and **phosphorescence** are all forms of luminescence or cold light.

CHEMICAL REACTION

Bioluminescence is created by a chemical reaction inside the body of a living thing. When certain chemicals mix together, they react to make light (see pages 28–29 for the recipe!).

Biofluorescence and **phosphorescence** are not chemical reactions. They both involve absorbing light from an outside source, like the sun, and using that to make light.

INCANDESCENCE IS LIGHT THAT COMES FROM HEAT

BIOLUMINESCENCE IS CREATED BY A CHEMICAL REACTION

LIGHT FROM AN OUTSIDE SOURCE

LIGHT GIVEN OFF AT LOWER ENERGY AND DIFFERENT COLOR

LIGHT ABSORBED BY SURFACE OF CREATURE

BIOFLUORESCENCE INVOLVES ABSORBING LIGHT

LIGHT IN, LIGHT OUT

Biofluorescence is common in marine animals that live in the upper ocean, like the yellow stingray. It is caused when light from the sun is absorbed by the surface of a creature's body. The surface absorbs the light and gives it off again. The light that is given off is a lower energy than the light that is absorbed— which makes it a different color. Biofluorescence stops as soon as the original light source stops, and we usually need special equipment to see it.

Phosphorescence is when a surface is charged up by a light source and gives off light for longer periods of time, even after the source of light stops shining. Glow-in-the-dark stickers are phosphorescent.

PLATE KEY

A SELECTION OF BIOFLUORESCENT SEA-DWELLERS

1. *HIPPOCAMPUS REIDI* SEAHORSE **2.** CHAIN CATSHARK **3.** FLOWER HAT JELLYFISH **4.** SHORTNOSE GREENEYE FISH
5. HAWKSBILL TURTLE **6.** YELLOW STINGRAY **7.** A VARIETY OF CORAL

A HIDDEN
WORLD OF LIGHT

SOME ANIMALS GLOW WITH A LIGHT THAT IS INVISIBLE TO HUMAN EYES
but technology can reveal these hidden sights for us.

CAN YOU SEE THE LIGHT?

Light travels in a wave pattern. The distance between waves of light is described as **wavelength**. We see different wavelengths of light as different colors.

The human eye can see a rainbow of wavelengths—but there are some wavelengths outside our range that we can't see. So how do humans know when something is secretly glowing?

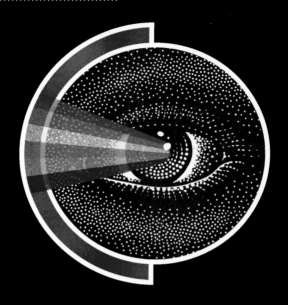

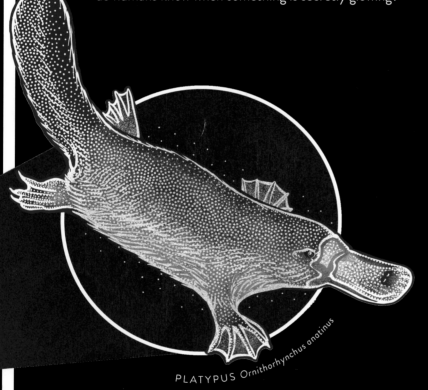

PLATYPUS *Ornithorhynchus anatinus*

MAKING THE INVISIBLE VISIBLE

A **biofluorescent** animal absorbs light and gives that light off again at a lower energy and a longer wavelength. This changes the light's color. The fluorescent light is so low energy that it is usually invisible to the human eye.

This changes when you shine a UV flashlight on a fluorescent animal. A UV flashlight shines UV (ultraviolet) light, which is very high energy. The animal's biofluorescence is supercharged by the high-energy UV light and shines it back out as a bright, visible light!

I'VE GOT A SECRET GLOW

Recently a variety of surprising furry friends have been discovered to glow under UV light. One of them is the platypus.

The platypus glows a luminous green/blue under UV light. Scientists aren't sure why, but they think it could be a kind of camouflage or that it might help a platypus to spot other platypuses under low light.

BIOLUMINESCENT HUMANS!

Humans also give off a small amount of **bioluminescence.** Our bioluminescence is much too weak for us to see but if it were stronger, we would be able to see ourselves glowing in the dark!

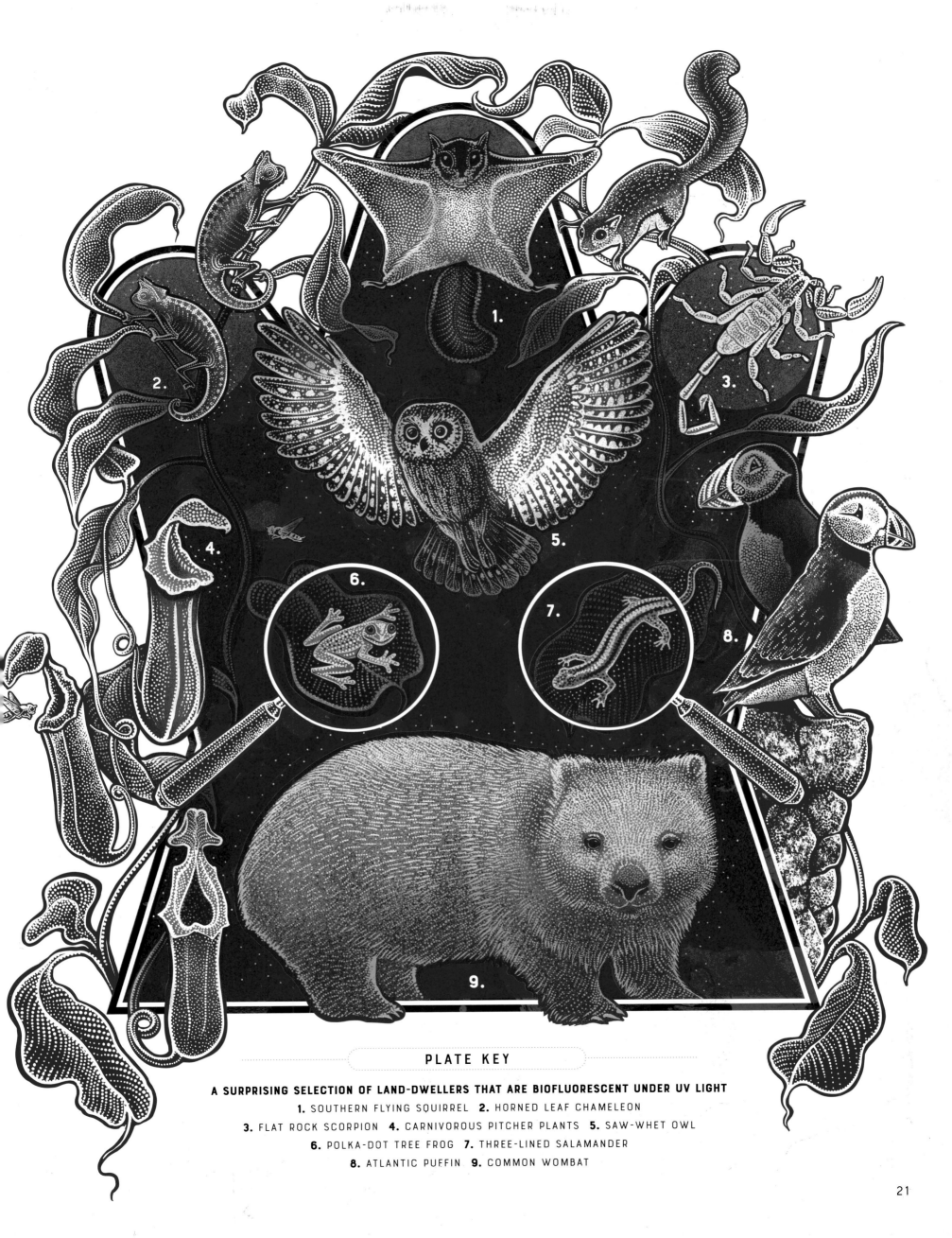

PLATE KEY

A SURPRISING SELECTION OF LAND-DWELLERS THAT ARE BIOFLUORESCENT UNDER UV LIGHT

1. SOUTHERN FLYING SQUIRREL **2.** HORNED LEAF CHAMELEON
3. FLAT ROCK SCORPION **4.** CARNIVOROUS PITCHER PLANTS **5.** SAW-WHET OWL
6. POLKA-DOT TREE FROG **7.** THREE-LINED SALAMANDER
8. ATLANTIC PUFFIN **9.** COMMON WOMBAT

THE ANATOMY OF BIOLUMINESCENCE

HOW IS IT POSSIBLE TO MAKE YOUR OWN LIGHT?

Many different creatures have evolved to become bioluminescent,
but not always in the same way. Here's how different creatures light up.

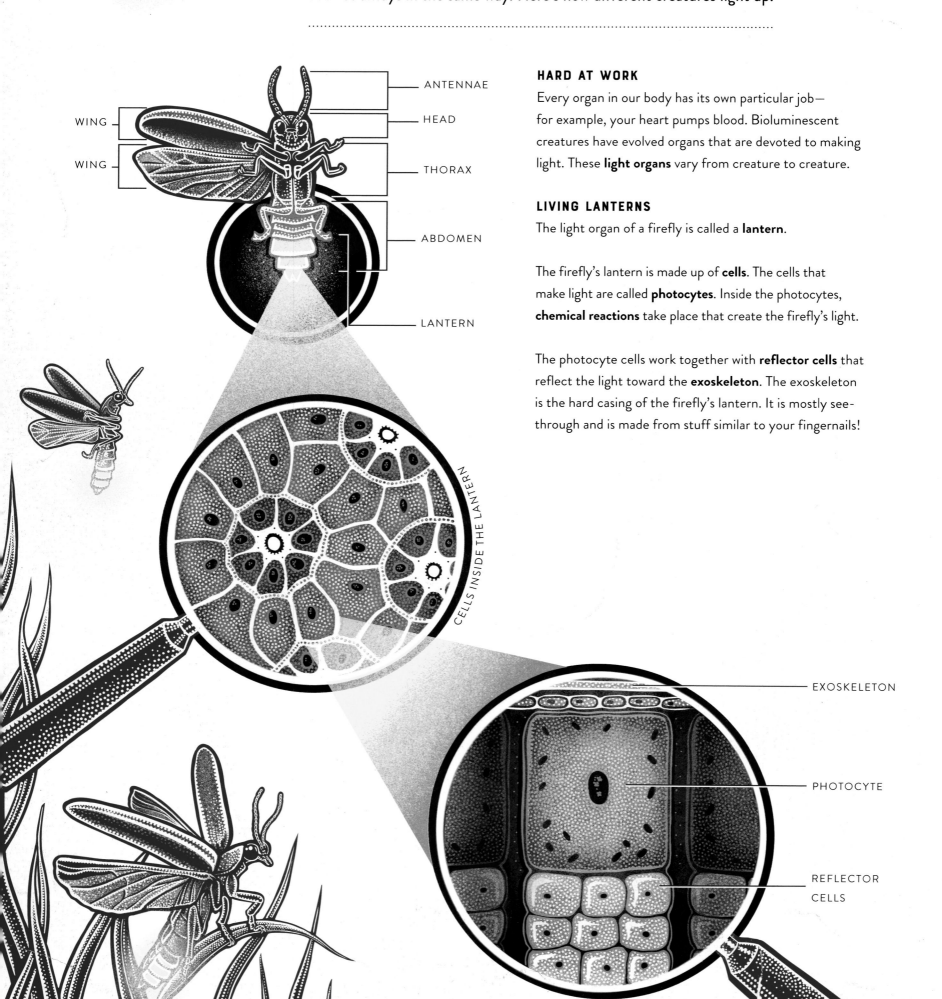

ANTENNAE

HEAD

WING

WING

THORAX

ABDOMEN

LANTERN

CELLS INSIDE THE LANTERN

EXOSKELETON

PHOTOCYTE

REFLECTOR
CELLS

HARD AT WORK

Every organ in our body has its own particular job—
for example, your heart pumps blood. Bioluminescent
creatures have evolved organs that are devoted to making
light. These **light organs** vary from creature to creature.

LIVING LANTERNS

The light organ of a firefly is called a **lantern**.

The firefly's lantern is made up of **cells**. The cells that
make light are called **photocytes**. Inside the photocytes,
chemical reactions take place that create the firefly's light.

The photocyte cells work together with **reflector cells** that
reflect the light toward the **exoskeleton**. The exoskeleton
is the hard casing of the firefly's lantern. It is mostly see-
through and is made from stuff similar to your fingernails!

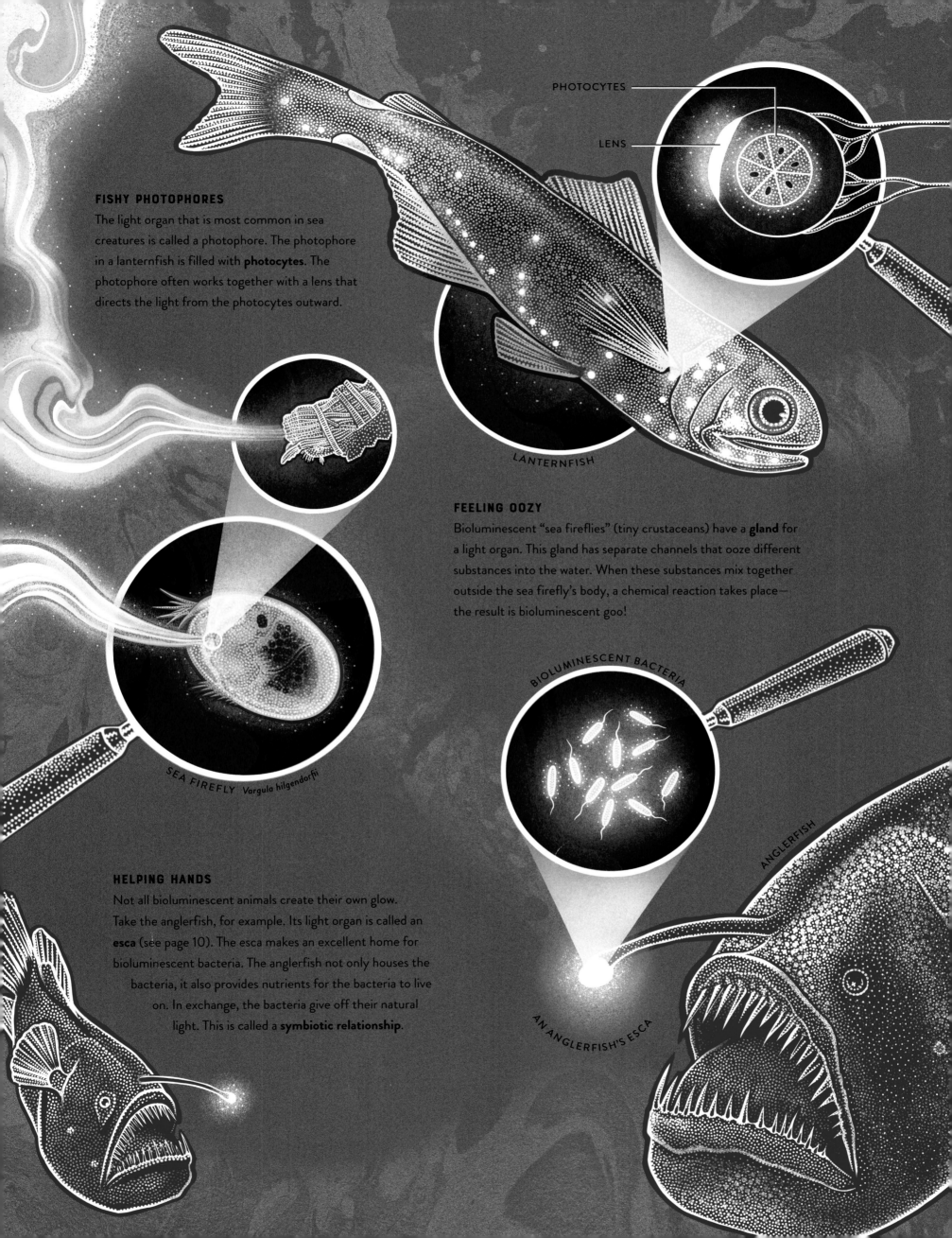

FISHY PHOTOPHORES

The light organ that is most common in sea creatures is called a photophore. The photophore in a lanternfish is filled with **photocytes**. The photophore often works together with a lens that directs the light from the photocytes outward.

PHOTOCYTES

LENS

LANTERNFISH

FEELING OOZY

Bioluminescent "sea fireflies" (tiny crustaceans) have a **gland** for a light organ. This gland has separate channels that ooze different substances into the water. When these substances mix together outside the sea firefly's body, a chemical reaction takes place—the result is bioluminescent goo!

SEA FIREFLY *Vargula hilgendorfii*

BIOLUMINESCENT BACTERIA

HELPING HANDS

Not all bioluminescent animals create their own glow. Take the anglerfish, for example. Its light organ is called an **esca** (see page 10). The esca makes an excellent home for bioluminescent bacteria. The anglerfish not only houses the bacteria, it also provides nutrients for the bacteria to live on. In exchange, the bacteria give off their natural light. This is called a **symbiotic relationship**.

ANGLERFISH

AN ANGLERFISH'S ESCA

THE DEEP DIVE

EVERYTHING WE KNOW ABOUT BIOLUMINESCENCE IS THANKS TO RESEARCHERS, scientists, and explorers. Some of them take great risks to go where no human has gone before—the bottom of the ocean! Did you know that less than 0.05% of the world's oceans have been explored?

EXPLORING THE DEEP OCEAN

Have you ever swum to the bottom of a pool and noticed the feeling of pressure on your ear drums? The deeper you dive, the more water there is pushing down on you. This is called **water pressure**. To discover and study the creatures dwelling in the depths of the ocean you need a vehicle that can deal with enormous water pressure. These vehicles are called **submersibles**. They are different from submarines because they are not designed to travel long distances through the ocean on their own—they are transported to their dive site by a ship.

Dr. Edith Widder is a deep-sea explorer, marine biologist, and expert on bioluminescence. Dr. Widder has been on many dives in deep-sea submersibles and was the first person to capture video of a giant squid in the deep sea. She and her team did this by creating their own deep-sea camera system. They attached the camera system to an E-jelly, a machine that mimics the wheel-like bioluminescence of an *Atolla* jellyfish. The giant squid was attracted to the E-jelly, allowing the team to observe it up close without disturbing it.

RESEARCHING IN LABORATORIES

You don't have to have good sea legs to be a bioluminescence expert! Much of the research on bioluminescence takes place in laboratories. This includes studying how, when, and why it happens, as well as exploring what we can do with this knowledge.

One biochemist, Dr. Emmett Chappelle, found a way to use the chemicals responsible for bioluminescence to detect **microorganisms** in water. We can also use this to test for life on other planets!

PRESERVING KNOWLEDGE AND EXPANDING MINDS IN MUSEUMS

Museums play an important role in passing on knowledge from one generation to the next. This includes taking care of the **specimens** that scientists have collected throughout history and making them available for everyone to study. Dr. Miranda Lowe is a **principal curator** at the Natural History Museum in London where she looks after the museum's collection of **Crustacea**. Dr. Lowe also works to raise awareness of the ways in which people of color have contributed to our knowledge of natural history.

EXPLORING ON LAND

In 2020, **mycologist** Dr. Samantha Karunarathna and his team identified a species of bioluminescent fungi in Meghalaya, India called *Roridomyces phyllostachydis*. The species was previously unknown to science—but that doesn't mean it was unknown to everyone!

Dr. Karunarathna's team learned about the species by asking local people if they knew of any bioluminescent fungi in the area. The answer was yes—it turned out people used the fungi-covered bamboo branches like glowing flashlights to navigate the forest at night.

HARNESSING
THE GLOW

BIOLUMINESCENCE HOLDS SO MUCH POTENTIAL for science, technology, and medicine. Scientists can work with the genes that cause luminescence and engineer them to be useful in many ways.

....

WHAT ARE GENES?

All living beings are the way they are because of **genes**. Each one is like a tiny biological instruction manual for how your body will grow and work.

Parents pass on genes to their children. If your parents are your blood relatives, it's likely that you look similar. For example, you might have brown eyes like your mother and black hair like your father.

Genes carry the ability to glow from one generation to the next. Scientists have discovered how to take the genes that make a creature bioluminescent or biofluorescent and put those genes into another creature to make it glow. It might sound like it belongs in a sci-fi movie but gene science is used in life-saving research and could shape the future of our world.

SUSTAINABLE STREET LIGHTS

In 2020, scientists found a way to use the genes from bioluminescent fungi to genetically engineer glowing plants. Bioluminescence is an extremely energy-efficient light source. With more glowing plants and fewer wasteful street lights, what could future streets and parks look like?

GENETIC HIGHLIGHTERS

The jellyfish *Aequorea victoria* is both bioluminescent *and* fluorescent. This means it can change the color of its glow from bright blue to neon green.

Scientists have discovered how to take the neon green gene from the *Aequorea victoria* jellyfish and "tag" it onto genes in other living things.

For example, when this gene is tagged onto a fur gene in another animal, the animal's fur will glow green under UV light.

Corals are another source of fluorescent genes and have an even wider range of colored genes. This "tagging" technique is useful in life-saving research!

DR. SIOUXSIE WILES *Founder of the Bioluminescent Superbugs Lab*

TRACKING AND TREATING

Dr. Siouxsie Wiles is the founder of the Bioluminescent Superbugs Lab. She and her team of researchers use bioluminescence to find cures for infectious diseases. They start by tagging bioluminescent genes onto the harmful bacteria that cause disease. The bacteria glow when they are alive and stop glowing when they are dead. Next the research team tests new medicines on the bacteria. If the bacteria stop glowing, the team knows the medicine works! This method is called **bioluminescent imaging**. It's been used to treat infectious diseases, to research cancer, and to learn more about disorders such as Alzheimer's disease.

TESTING FOR POLLUTION

We can also use bioluminescent bacteria to check for **pollution** in water. Scientists bring mud from a riverbed to the lab and mix it with bioluminescent bacteria. The glowing bacteria will start to fade if the muddy water is polluted. The faster the light fades, the faster the bacteria are being killed by toxic chemicals in the water.

THE RECIPE FOR LIGHT

A LITTLE OF THIS, A LITTLE OF THAT . . . BOOM!

Bioluminescence is caused by a chemical reaction.
For the reaction to take place, you need the right ingredients
and the right recipe. Here is a sea firefly's recipe for light.

THE SEA FIREFLY

LIGHT SHOW

A sea firefly is a tiny **crustacean** about the size of a
sesame seed. It whizzes around in the ocean, releasing
bioluminescent goo whenever it is disturbed. It also
puts on beautiful light displays when it wants to attract
a mate, leaving upward trails of beaded light in the
ocean. Exactly how does a sea firefly create these
magical displays? Chemistry!

SEA FIREFLY *Vargula hilgendorfii*

THE INGREDIENTS

The sea firefly's recipe for bioluminescence combines two similar-
sounding ingredients—**luciferin** and **luciferase**—with **oxygen**.
Luciferin and luciferase are both stored inside the sea firefly's
body. Oxygen is in the ocean water.

THE METHOD

Like all recipes, the ingredients need to be combined using a
special method. The sea firefly's method is to squirt luciferin out
of a **gland** on one side of its body and luciferase out of a gland
on the other side of its body. Once they are in the water, both
ingredients react with each other and oxygen.

THE RESULT

Luciferase binds the luciferin and oxygen together, a little like how
eggs bind sugar and flour together in a cake. When they are bound
together, they create something called **oxyluciferin**. When
oxyluciferin is made, it has too much energy at first and needs
to release it. It releases that energy in the form of light!

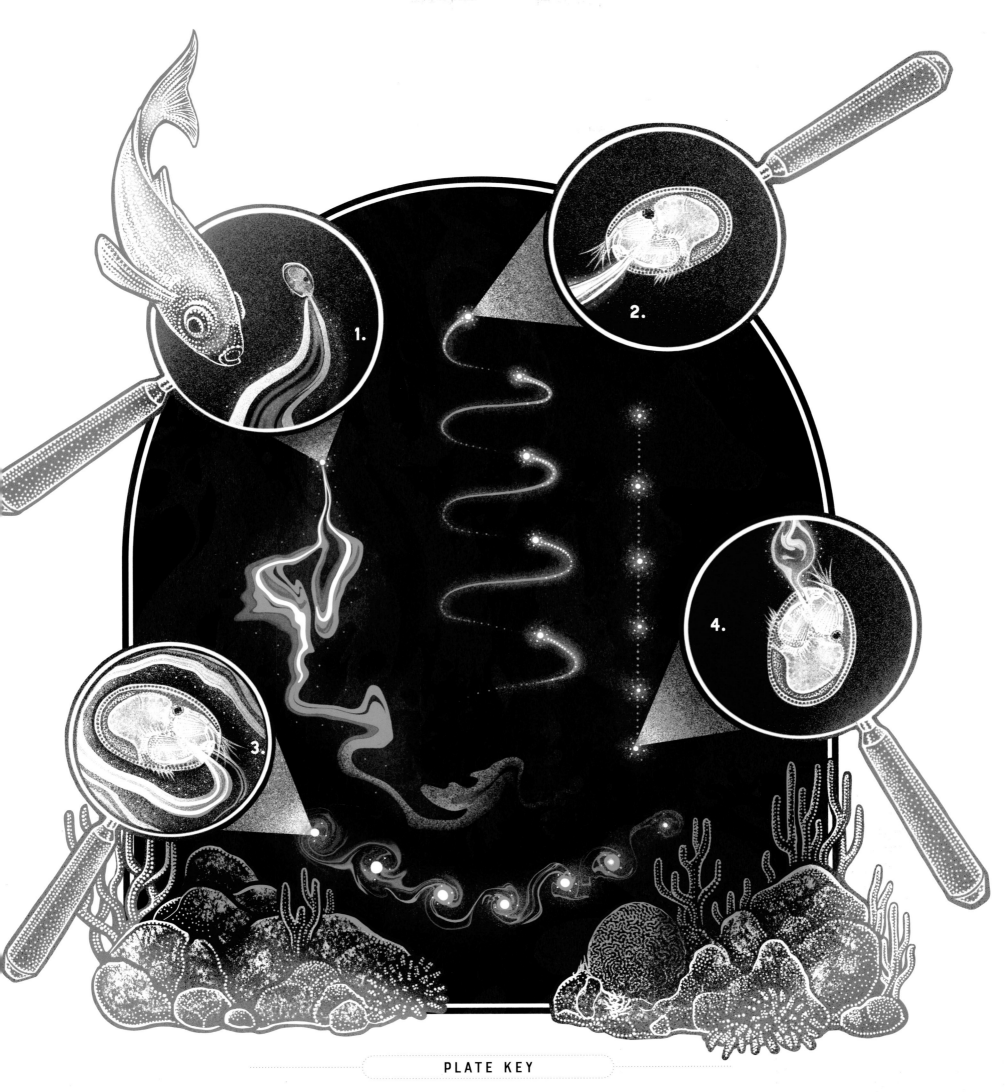

PLATE KEY

DIFFERENT SPECIES OF SEA FIREFLIES HAVE DIFFERENT FLASH PATTERNS
1. MOST SPECIES USE BIOLUMINESCENCE TO PUT OFF PREDATORS, WITH LONG, CHAOTIC SWIRLS
SOME SPECIES USE THEIR BIOLUMINESCENCE TO ATTRACT A MATE
2. *PHOTEROS ANNECOHENAE* MOSTLY SWOOP UPWARD **3.** *MARISTELLA CHICOI* USE LONG, HORIZONTAL
PULSES THAT LINGER IN THE WATER **4.** *PHOTEROS MORINI* USE QUICK DOWNWARD FLASHES

BRIGHT FUTURE

THE WONDERS OF BIOLUMINESCENCE ARE AWE-INSPIRING, BUT BIOLUMINESCENT FORMS OF LIFE are facing many challenges. Our planet is getting warmer and habitats are under threat due to climate change. It's essential for us all to stay optimistic and work together toward a brighter future.

SHARE THE WONDER!

Spend some time learning about nature and observing it. Then tell people about the wonderful things you've seen— it will help spread the message that nature is worth protecting.

Become a **citizen scientist** and join a group that counts fireflies and glowworms in your area. The information that citizen scientists collect can help show why certain species and habitats need our protection.

BECOME A CITIZEN SCIENTIST

ATTEND A STAR COUNT

TURN OFF THE LIGHTS

Light pollution leads to falling numbers of fireflies and glowworms. However, light pollution is quite simple to fix—you can help by turning off any lights that you're not using at night! Reducing light pollution makes an immediate difference to nocturnal wildlife. Why not write to your local representative to see what they are doing to cut down on light pollution?

Some communities hold annual **star counts** to keep track of light pollution. The darker the sky and the more stars you can count, the less light pollution there is!

CAMPAIGN FOR OUR OCEANS

ONLY 1 EARTH

END OFFSHORE DRILLING!

YOUTH STRIKE FOR CLIMATE

STOP ECOCIDE!

SAVE OUR OCEANS

STOP OCEAN PLASTIC

CAMPAIGN FOR OUR OCEANS

Our oceans face lots of challenges, including plastic pollution and overfishing. Increasing levels of the gas **carbon dioxide** are causing **coral bleaching** and are destroying reef habitats. We can help by **campaigning** for the government to invest in **renewable energy sources**, as well as by eating less fish and reducing how much plastic and energy we use.

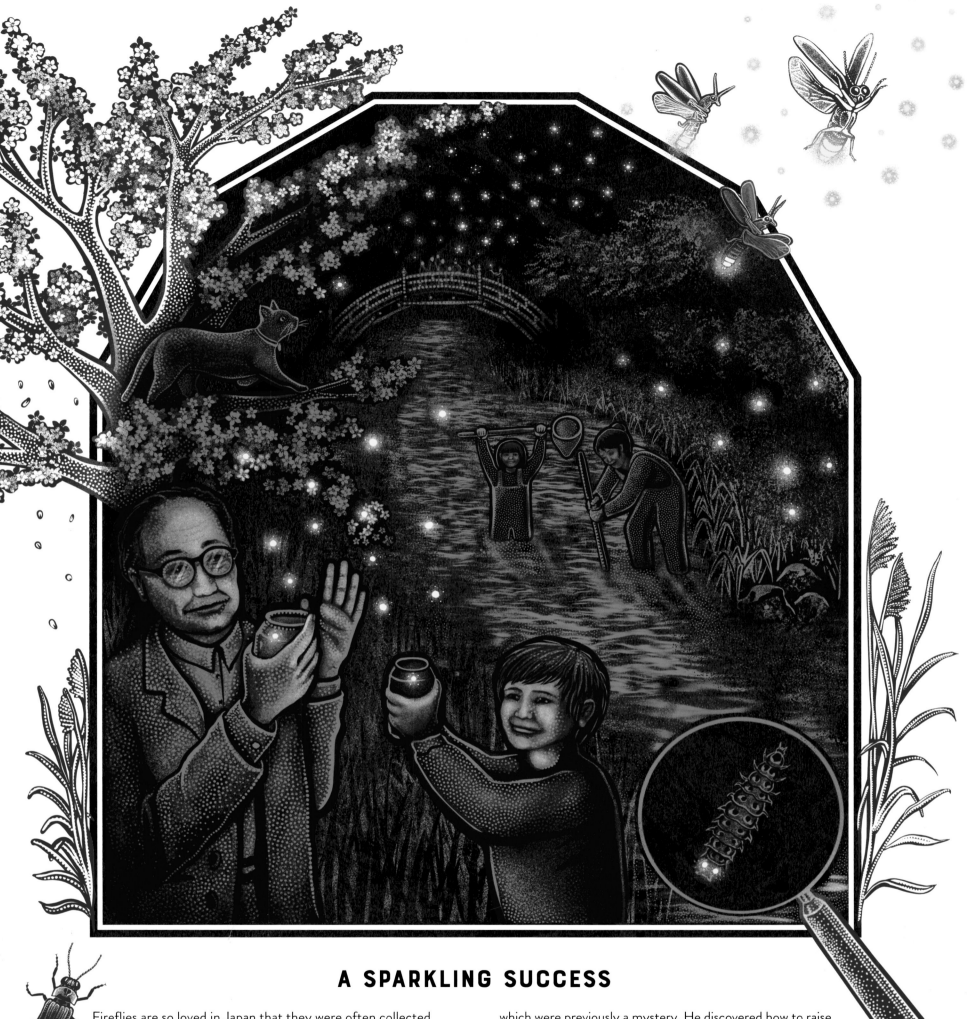

A SPARKLING SUCCESS

Fireflies are so loved in Japan that they were often collected from rural areas and sold to people in the cities to enjoy. This became a problem because the fireflies needed the rivers of their wild habitat to survive. At the same time, rivers were being polluted. By the 1920s, the firefly population in Japan was worryingly low.

Luckily, a firefly fan named Kiichiro Minami came to the rescue. He studied the life cycle and eating habits of the firefly, which were previously a mystery. He discovered how to raise fireflies in captivity and increase their population. Members of the community helped by cleaning up local rivers so that the fireflies could thrive there once again. The Japanese government banned businesses from collecting and selling fireflies. The fireflies now have a stable population. The story of these fireflies shows how individuals, communities, and governments can work together to make a difference.

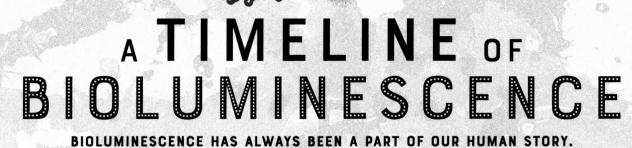

A TIMELINE OF BIOLUMINESCENCE

BIOLUMINESCENCE HAS ALWAYS BEEN A PART OF OUR HUMAN STORY.

BCE stands for "Before the Common Era," and CE stands for "Common Era."
The Common Era starts at year 1. Events that occurred before then are counted back from year 1.

THE OLDEST WRITTEN RECORDS
AROUND 1500 TO 1000 BCE

The oldest written mentions of luminous animals are found in ancient Chinese poetry. It is thought that they refer to fireflies!

FIREFLIES AND DINOSAURS
CRETACEOUS PERIOD
144 MILLION BCE TO 65 MILLION BCE

In 2021, a fossil of an early ancestor of the firefly was found in northern Myanmar. This fossil proved that they existed during the Cretaceous period, along with many dinosaurs! There were also bioluminescent fish in this time period—the oldest of these were probably ancestors of the dragonfish.

FOLKLORE & LEGENDS

Many stories about glowing animals have been passed down through the generations. In Japanese folklore, fireflies, called *hotaru*, are believed to be the souls of warriors killed in battle.

Fireflies are also present in Native American stories. There is an Apache legend that describes how fire began with fireflies. It belonged only to them—until a clever trickster fox stole some of their fire and spread it across the land.

GLOWING GREEKS
AROUND 550 BCE TO 300 BCE

The ancient Greek scholar Anaximenes recorded descriptions of sea sparkle. He wrote that sailors sometimes saw the sea light up when it was disturbed by oars and boats. They called this light the "Wheels of Poseidon." Poseidon was the Greek god of the sea, who was said to ride a chariot pulled by horses with the tails of fish!

Aristotle, an ancient Greek philosopher, described damp wood that glowed in the dark, and also wrote about sea sparkle, which he described as "exhalations of fire". He called it "cold light" because he noticed that it does not produce heat like a fire or candle.

RAVING ROMANS AND MESSY MEALS
AROUND 50 CE

Pliny the Elder was a Roman scholar who wrote about several bioluminescent species in his work *Naturalis Historia*. He had the idea of smearing a jellyfish on his cane so that it could also be used as a torch!

He also recorded a bioluminescent shellfish called the piddock, which oozes blue glowing goo when chewed. This was apparently very funny to the Romans, who loved to hold late-night feasts and eat lots of raw shellfish— the glowing "juice" went everywhere!

MEDIEVAL MANUSCRIPTS
AROUND 500 TO 1400S CE

In medieval times, scholars would handwrite and draw books that included both real animals and mythical beasts. These books are called **bestiaries**.

One 13th-century bestiary, *De Animalibus*, was written by Albertus Magnus, a German monk. The book included descriptions of glowing species that had not been recorded before.

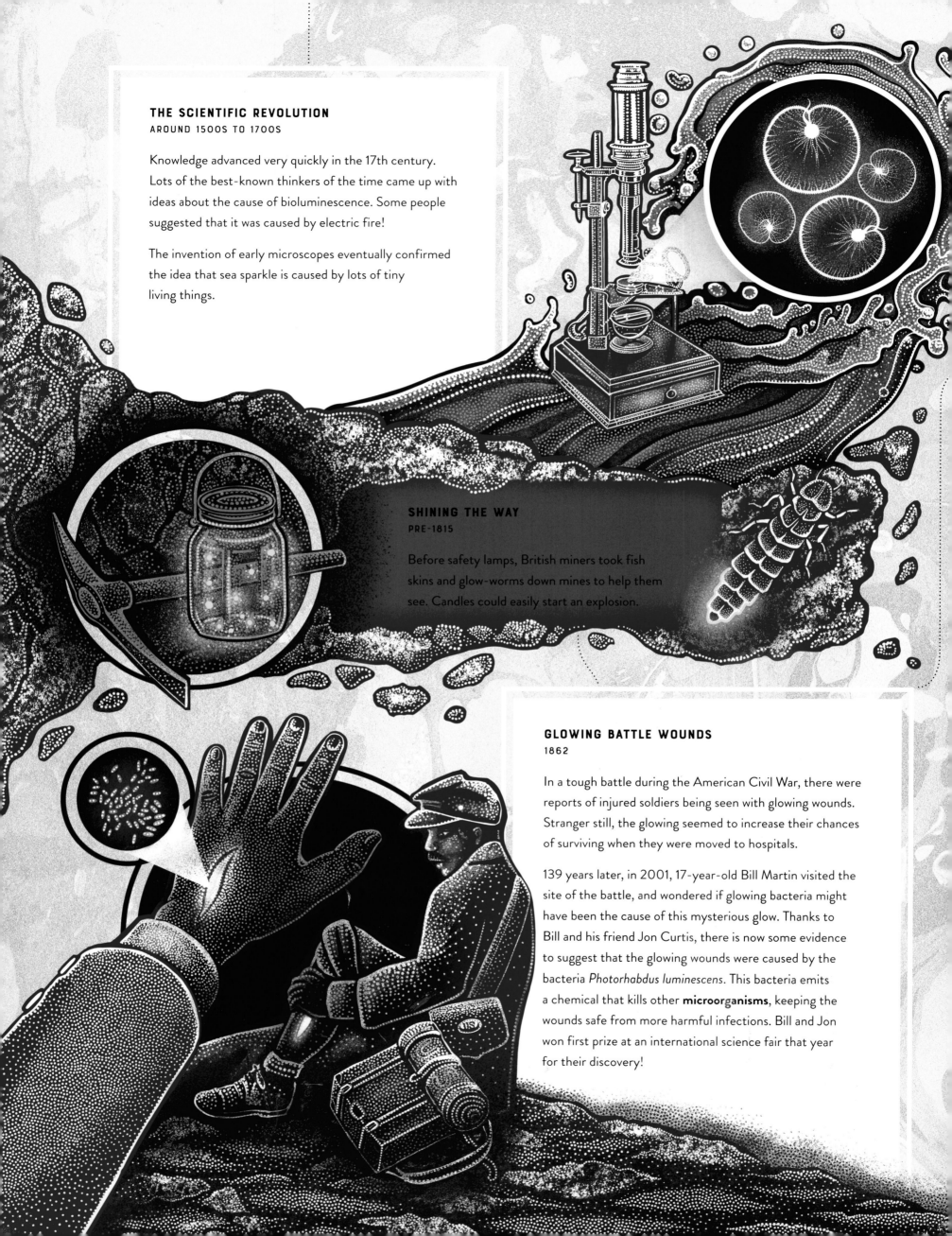

THE SCIENTIFIC REVOLUTION
AROUND 1500S TO 1700S

Knowledge advanced very quickly in the 17th century. Lots of the best-known thinkers of the time came up with ideas about the cause of bioluminescence. Some people suggested that it was caused by electric fire!

The invention of early microscopes eventually confirmed the idea that sea sparkle is caused by lots of tiny living things.

SHINING THE WAY
PRE-1815

Before safety lamps, British miners took fish skins and glow-worms down mines to help them see. Candles could easily start an explosion.

GLOWING BATTLE WOUNDS
1862

In a tough battle during the American Civil War, there were reports of injured soldiers being seen with glowing wounds. Stranger still, the glowing seemed to increase their chances of surviving when they were moved to hospitals.

139 years later, in 2001, 17-year-old Bill Martin visited the site of the battle, and wondered if glowing bacteria might have been the cause of this mysterious glow. Thanks to Bill and his friend Jon Curtis, there is now some evidence to suggest that the glowing wounds were caused by the bacteria *Photorhabdus luminescens*. This bacteria emits a chemical that kills other **microorganisms**, keeping the wounds safe from more harmful infections. Bill and Jon won first prize at an international science fair that year for their discovery!

A BIOCHEMISTRY BREAKTHROUGH
1885

Raphaël Dubois extracted chemicals responsible for bioluminescence. He named them **luciferin** and **luciferase**.

WORLD WAR I
1914–1918

Soldiers in the trenches sometimes used glowworms to read maps without drawing dangerous attention to themselves.

Bioluminescence also helped the British Navy to sink a German submarine. Plankton created a glowing wake that was bright enough to give away the submarine's position.

THE FIRST DEEP-SEA DIVE
1930 CE

Otis Barton and Will Beebe made the first deep dive in an early submersible, called a **bathysphere**. A phoneline was attached so they could report their findings. Else Bostelmann, a scientific illustrator, created drawings based on Beebe's descriptions. Her drawings brought previously unseen deep-sea creatures to life.

WORLD WAR II
1939–1945

It is said that Japanese soldiers carried dried sea fireflies into battle at night. Ground up in water, they gave off enough light to read maps in the dark, without being seen by the enemy.

THE STORY CONTINUES . . .
The late 20th and 21st centuries brought many breakthroughs in our knowledge of bioluminescence, but there is still lots more to find out!

A MAP OF BIOLUMINESCENCE

BIOLUMINESCENCE CAN BE SEEN ALL OVER THE WORLD. HERE ARE SOME EXAMPLES—THEY MIGHT BE CLOSER TO HOME THAN YOU THINK!

LUMINOUS MILLIPEDES *California*

MARINE WORMS *Jersey*

COMB JELLIES *United States*

BIOLUMINESCENT BAYS *Puerto Rico*

RAILROAD GLOWWORM *Brazil*

CLICK BEETLE *Brazil*

LUMINOUS MILLIPEDES

Millipedes from the family *Motyxia* glow a bright blue-green, and can be found in the Sierra Nevada mountains. They glow to warn predators of their deadly secret—they are **toxic**, and will spray cyanide at their attackers!

THE AMAZON RAINFOREST

The Amazon is home to many species that cannot be found anywhere else in the world, including bioluminescent ones! Click beetle larvae light up termite mounds. Railroad glowworms are named for their rows of lights, which look like the windows on a train—they even have little red headlamps. Bioluminescent fungi can also be seen there, such as *Neonothopanus gardneri*.

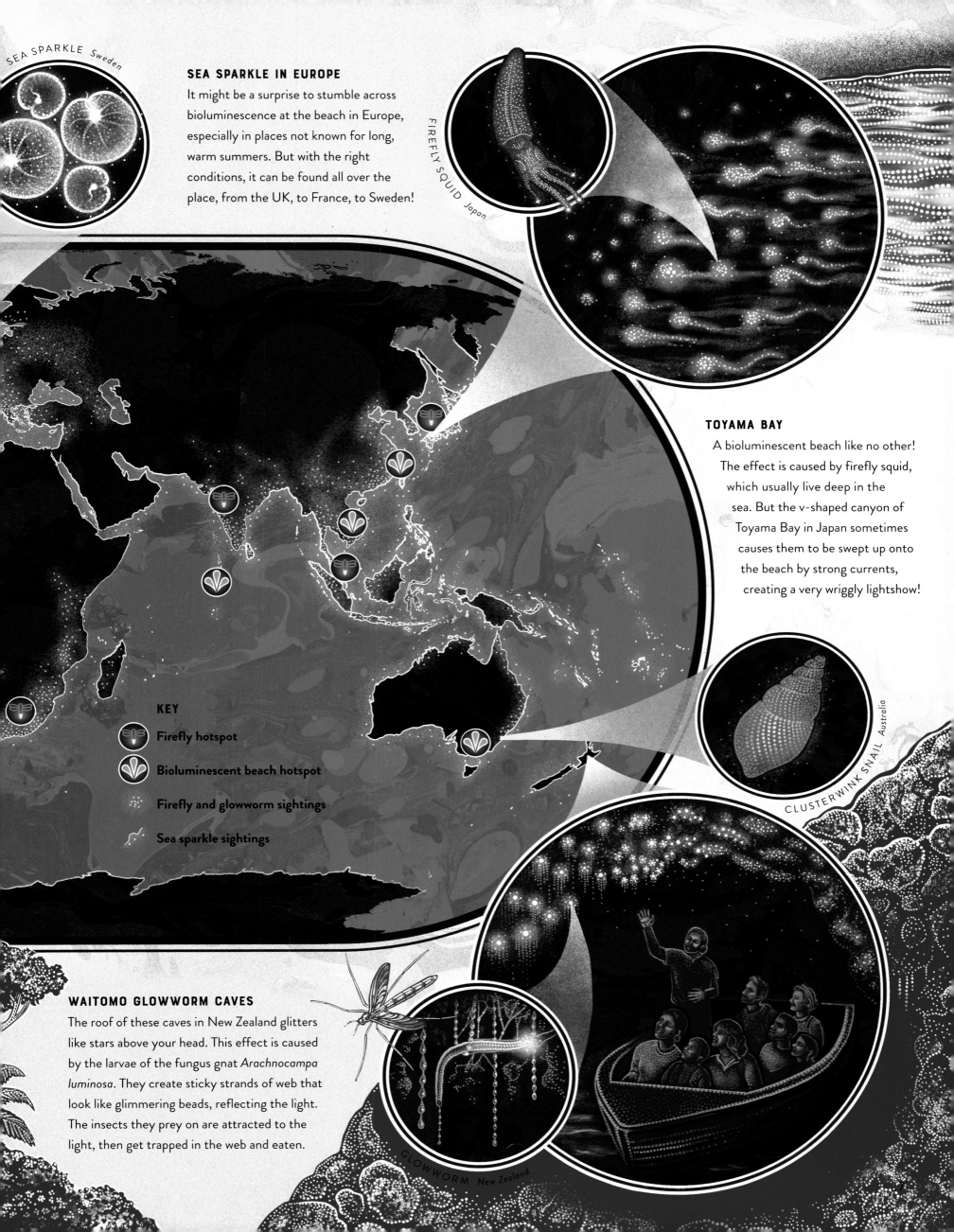

SEA SPARKLE Sweden

SEA SPARKLE IN EUROPE

It might be a surprise to stumble across bioluminescence at the beach in Europe, especially in places not known for long, warm summers. But with the right conditions, it can be found all over the place, from the UK, to France, to Sweden!

FIREFLY SQUID Japan

TOYAMA BAY

A bioluminescent beach like no other! The effect is caused by firefly squid, which usually live deep in the sea. But the v-shaped canyon of Toyama Bay in Japan sometimes causes them to be swept up onto the beach by strong currents, creating a very wriggly lightshow!

CLUSTERWINK SNAIL Australia

KEY

⬤ **Firefly hotspot**

⬤ **Bioluminescent beach hotspot**

Firefly and glowworm sightings

Sea sparkle sightings

WAITOMO GLOWWORM CAVES

The roof of these caves in New Zealand glitters like stars above your head. This effect is caused by the larvae of the fungus gnat *Arachnocampa luminosa*. They create sticky strands of web that look like glimmering beads, reflecting the light. The insects they prey on are attracted to the light, then get trapped in the web and eaten.

GLOWWORM New Zealand

GLOSSARY

adapt When a creature becomes better suited to its environment to improve its chances of survival.

bestiary A book filled with descriptions of real and mythical animals.

biofluorescence When the surface of a creature's body absorbs light from the sun and gives it off again. This effect stops as soon as the original light source stops.

bioluminescence Light that is produced by living things.

bioluminescent imaging A way of using bioluminescence to track disease or the effects of a medicine or other treatment.

campaigning Using organized actions to achieve a goal or promote a cause.

carbon dioxide A gas that is naturally present in the Earth's atmosphere. Industrial pollution causes the level of carbon dioxide to rise, and this can be harmful to the environment.

cell A tiny structure that all living things are made of.

chemical reaction An effect that occurs when two or more chemicals are mixed together.

citizen scientist A member of the public who records information and helps with scientific research.

coral bleaching Coral is a colony of tiny invertebrate animals that live together under the sea. When the coral is damaged by pollution, disease, or conditions that are too warm, it turns white. This is called bleaching.

crustacean An invertebrate animal with a tough exoskeleton and jointed legs. This family of creatures is known as *Crustacea* and includes crabs, shrimp, and lobsters.

curator Someone who is in charge of the collections in a museum.

dinoflagellate A type of single-cell sea plankton. Some species of dinoflagellate create the glittering lights known as "sea sparkle."

esca The light organ of an anglerfish, which they use to lure their prey.

exoskeleton The hard outer casing of an insect or other invertebrate's body.

fruiting body The rounded top part of a mushroom, where spores are produced.

gene A set of instructions carried inside the nucleus of a cell. These instructions tell the cell how to grow and what to do.

gland A group of cells inside a living thing that make substances that the animal or plant needs.

hyphae Stringy fibers inside a mushroom.

illicium The scientific name for the "fishing rod" that supports the light of an anglerfish.

incandescence Light that is created by heat.

invertebrate An animal without a backbone.

lantern The light organ of insects such as fireflies and glowworms.

larva The young form of an insect. The plural is larvae.

light organ A part of an animal's body that creates light.

light pollution Pollution caused by too many artificial lights, which means that stars in the night sky aren't visible.

luciferase A substance produced in bioluminescent animals. It is combined with luciferin and oxygen to make light.

luciferin A chemical produced in bioluminescent animals. It is combined with luciferase and oxygen to make light. Luciferase causes the reaction without being changed itself.

luminescence Light that is made without heat.

mate A partner for the purposes of reproducing.

microorganism A living thing that is too small to see with the naked eye.

midnight zone The part of the sea that's more than 3,300 feet deep.

migration A journey made by an animal or bird to another place where the weather is warmer or food is easier to find.

mucus A slimy liquid produced by living things.

mycelium The root-like network formed by the hyphae of a mushroom or other fungus.

mycologist A scientist who studies fungi.

nocturnal An animal that is nocturnal is active at night and often sleeps during the day.

nucleus The part of a cell that contains its genes and controls its growth and reproduction.

oxygen A chemical element that is vital to living things.

oxyluciferin A chemical created by combining oxygen and luciferin. When it is made, light energy is released.

phosphorescence Light created by shining a light source on a surface, which is then charged up and gives off light of its own, even after the original source of light stops shining.

photocyte A cell that produces light.

photophore A gland on the body of a fish or other sea creature that produces light.

pollution Damage to the environment caused by harmful substances.

predator An animal that hunts other animals to eat.

prey An animal that is hunted and eaten by other animals.

reflector cell A cell found inside the lantern of an insect, which reflects the light created by photocytes.

renewable energy sources Sources of energy that can be used repeatedly and will be naturally replaced, including wind, water, and solar power.

specimen A sample of a particular substance or species that is collected and studied by scientists.

star count A survey in which people count the stars that they can see in the night sky. It is a good way of keeping track of light pollution.

submersible A small undersea vehicle often used for scientific research.

sunlight zone The part of the sea from the water's surface down to 650 feet deep.

swarm A large group of insects.

symbiotic relationship or **symbiosis** A relationship that has evolved between two different animals or plants, in which they both benefit from living together.

thallus The stalk of a mushroom.

toxic Containing natural poisons called toxins, which are produced in the bodies of some living things.

twilight zone The part of the sea between 650 and 3,300 feet deep.

water pressure The force of water pushing downward. The deeper you go into the water, the higher the water pressure.

wavelength The distance between waves of light. Humans see light of different wavelengths as different colors.

SEA SPARKLE SPOTTING
If you are lucky enough to see sea sparkle in the waves one day, make sure to follow local advice as to whether it's safe to swim!

FIREFLY FREEDOM!
It can be tempting to capture wild fireflies and admire their glow close up, but they're much happier flying free than being trapped in a jar. If you do catch any, make sure they have plenty of air and release them soon after, in the same place you found them.

INDEX